A little book

Hampshire

Personal memories inspired by The Francis Frith Collection®

THE FRANCIS FRITH COLLECTION

www.francisfrith.com

Based on a book first published in the United Kingdom in 2013 by The Francis Frith Collection®

This edition published exclusively for Bradwell Books in 2013
For trade enquiries see: www.bradwellbooks.com or tel: 0800 834 920
ISBN 978-1-84589-738-3

British Library Cataloguing in Publication Data

A Little Book of Hampshire Memories
Personal Memories inspired by the Francis Frith Collection

The Francis Frith Collection
6 Oakley Business Park,
Wylye Road, Dinton,
Wiltshire SP3 5EU
Tel: +44 (0) 1722 716 376
Email: info@francisfrith.co.uk
www.francisfrith.com

Printed and bound in Malaysia
Contains material sourced from responsibly managed forests

Front Cover: New Forest Ponies, Bucklers Hard c1960 B43063p
Frontispiece: Odiham, High Street c1950 O8007x

The colour-tinting is for illustrative purposes only, and is not intended to be historically accurate

AS WITH ANY HISTORICAL DATABASE, THE FRANCIS FRITH ARCHIVE IS CONSTANTLY BEING
CORRECTED AND IMPROVED, AND THE PUBLISHERS WOULD WELCOME INFORMATION ON
OMISSIONS OR INACCURACIES

A little book of Memories – A Dedication

This book has been compiled from a selection of the thousands of personal memories added by visitors to the Frith website and could not have happened without these contributions. We are very grateful to everyone who has taken the time to share their memories in this way. This book is dedicated to everyone who has taken the time to participate in the Frith Memories project.

It is comforting to find so many stories full of human warmth which bring back happy memories of "the good old days". We hope that everyone reading this book will find stories that amuse and fascinate whilst at the same time be reminded of why we feel affection for Britain and what makes us all British.

Francis Frith always expressed the wish that his photographs be made available to as wide an audience as possible and so it is particularly pleasing to me that by creating the Frith web site we have been able to make this nationally important photographic record of Britain available to a worldwide audience. Now, by providing the Share Your Memories feature on the website we are delighted to provide an opportunity for members of the public to record their own stories and to see them published (both on the website and in this book), ensuring that they are shared and not lost or forgotten.

We hope that you too will be motivated to visit our website and add your own memories to this growing treasure trove – helping us to make it an even more comprehensive record of the changes that have taken place in Britain in the last 100 years and a resource that will be valued by generations to come.

John M Buck
Managing Director
www.francisfrith.com

A little book of memories

This was our favourite spot on the beach

This 1890 photograph was taken at about the same place on the pebbled Southsea Beach where our family always established their bit of 'turf' in the 1950s. There was a whole ritual to it – setting up the blanket so it wouldn't get blown out to sea, then arranging the baskets of delicious ham sandwiches and bottles of home-made ginger ale we had brought with us. My step-father always had The Times newspaper or a Penguin book at hand whilst my step-grandfather, Pop, smoked his pipe and Mum knitted.

On this beach I once dug up a fully loaded revolver. When I showed it to my step-grandfather he grabbed it out of my hand and tossed it angrily out to sea for some other kid to find and shoot himself with, no doubt!

Our family was maniacal about swimming here in freezing, blustery April weather when no one else with a grain of sense was on the beach…but there we sat, blown all to hell by the cold wind, and into the water went I, whether I wanted to or not. Upon emerging after the Obligatory 'dip' (as soon as I could get away with it) the blood in the backs of my hands would have separated into blue and red blotches. I have rarely been so bitterly, miserably cold!   *Dylan Rivis*

SOUTHSEA, The Beach and Clarence Pier 1890 22761

Only the British would enjoy this!

Reading the memory on the Frith website from Dylan Rivis (opposite) about visits to Southsea beach on cold days in April struck a chord with me. My mum came from Southsea, so many day trips and holidays were spent on Eastney beach. Brrr! My dad usually lay on the pebbles dressed up to his overcoat, managing to escape the worst of the wind that way. I adored swimming in the sea, but getting dry and dressed was nearly impossible with those white-numb fingers. Still, we all warmed up with a brisk walk along the prom.

Frances Golynia

"On this beach I once dug up a fully loaded revolver. When I showed it to my step-grandfather he grabbed it out of my hand and tossed it angrily out to sea."

A little book of memories

My piano lessons on Newbury Road

I was 9 when this photo was taken of Newbury Road in Kingsclere, north-west of Basingstoke. I used to walk from my house on Coppice Road to Newbury Road where I took piano lessons. I don't remember the name of the teacher but she also played the organ at St Mary's Church in the village, and she was the sister of Mrs Fred Hopkins, who owned the store on George Street. Her black spaniel always sprawled over my feet while I played. I think that's the reason why I always play the piano with the 'loud' pedal! I enjoyed looking at the photos of Kingsclere on the Frith website, because I now live in Mississippi in the USA and I haven't been back there for over 40 years.

Susan Dunn

Kingsclere, Newbury Road c1955 K140023

The bed-bug weathervane!

St Mary's Church at Kingsclere is famous for a most unusual decoration, a weather-vane in the shape of a bed-bug, seen on the left-hand side of the tower in this view. It is a very tasteful bed-bug, with six little crosses for legs, and another for its tail. The story goes that back in the early 13th century King John was hunting in the area. A thick fog prevented him returning to his hunting lodge on Cottington Hill and he had to spend the night at the local inn in Kingsclere, where his rest was much disturbed by the depredations of bed-bugs upon the royal person. King John was so annoyed by his disturbed night that he ordered an effigy of a bed-bug to be erected on the church tower, and a depiction of the insect remains there to this day.

Julia Skinner

Kingsclere, St Mary's Church c1960 K140081

When the Flying Scotsman came through Bramley Station

I think it was 1963 when the Flying Scotsman steam train came through Bramley station. I was only small at the time. We all gathered to watch it come through at a fantastic speed, and I remember the station master, Jimmy Seagull, telling us kids to stand well back, as the force of the train passing was likely to suck us off the platform if we got too close! We saw lots of steam trains in those days, but rarely one as famous as that.

On the left of this photograph is Hanmore's bakers and grocers shop, we used to get a chocolate Raspberry Ruffle every time we went in there. I also remember an occasion when the butcher next door hung my rag doll on one of his spikes when I took her into his shop!

Angela Swords

Bramley, The Level Crossing c1960 B696026

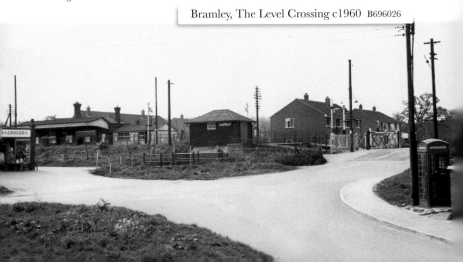

Working at the Hampshire Chronicle newspaper

In the early 1960s I started work at the old Hampshire Chronicle offices in Winchester's High Street (the current Chronicle premises at Winchester are in Upper Brook Street). I began my journalist career as a cub reporter under the benign eye of Monica Woodhouse and news editor 'Jock' Coutts. It was a great place to be. We reported on every court from magistrates to assizes, every council from parish to county, we did passing-out parades at the Green Jackets' barracks, and Winchester has a cathedral, a public school, a prison – all human life is there! I was truly 'educated' at Winchester and it was in the city that I met the girl who became my wife. The Chronicle in those days was still produced using a 'hot metal' process, as were most newspapers at that time, little changed from the 15th century when William Caxton introduced the printing press into England. In one lifetime we've gone from Caxton to computers – and the old Chronicle offices at 57 High Street now house an Italian restaurant. Time passes so quickly.

David Stuckey

Winchester, High Street 1928 80886

Memories of Sherfield on Loddon in the 1960s

It was lovely to come across the photos of Sherfield on Loddon on the Frith website. We lived there from 1961 to 1969 and my parents ran the village store (known then as The Stores) seen on the left of this view, which was taken from outside our shop. I have lots of memories from those days as a teenager. We would use that phone-box in the picture to tap out numbers and get calls for free. On Saturday mornings I worked in the shop (the pay was 2/6 per hour). We cut our own cheese and bacon and wrapped them in greaseproof paper. When I first moved there we gave customers individual service, but we converted to self-service later. We sold all sorts of things including paraffin and wellie-boots.

Sherfield on Loddon, The Village c1955 s631002

On Saturday afternoons we watched the local lads playing football on the common whilst listening to Radio Caroline on our transistor radios. In those days the main Basingstoke to Reading road ran right through the village. I remember sitting on a bench under one of the old horse-chestnut trees opposite the Four Horseshoes pub with some of the local kids. We knew lots of people because of running the shop and we also did a delivery round to Wildmoor and other out-of-the-way places.

Chrissie Ferngrove

> "On Saturday afternoons we watched the local lads playing football on the common whilst listening to Radio Caroline on our transistor radios."

Sherfield on Loddon, Bramley Road and the Four Horseshoes c1955 S631011

9

A little book of memories

Life at Greywell in the 1950s

My family lived at 4 Vine Cottages at Greywell (near Odiham) for a few years in the 1950s, my father worked for Lord Dorchester on the farm there. In 1953 I recall going to a party in the village hall to celebrate the Coronation of Queen Elizabeth II, where we were all given a coin and a commemorative mug. One year there was a May Fair and a maypole was erected in the village which I danced around with other children. We left the village for Rowlands Castle but returned there again in 1958. My father worked again for Lord Dorchester, however this time we lived in the house on Greywell Hill Farm instead of in the village. We were sure the house was haunted as we could hear noises in the bedroom. We had a lot of strange things happen while living there.

I remember the snowdrops were wonderful and grew in great clumps in our garden. Over the fence was a mesh-wired building that was used to hang the pheasant, deer and rabbit that were shot on the farm. My father had an old tobacco tin which held mole tails, he was paid for every mole he caught in the big house lawn. I was allowed to fill the thick-lipped milk bottles in the dairy and had a favourite cow called Fairy, I would sit in the manger and talk to her while she was being milked.

I recall my mother cleaning at the big house (Greywell Hill) and I went with her. I wandered the house and there was an incident one day when I opened a door to a bathroom where Lady Dorchester was taking a bath – oops.

Strange how I remember the sun always seemed to be shining back in those days. *Patrice Amor*

Happy memories of King George V Park in Farnborough

I have lovely memories of this park in all seasons – the piles of leaves in the autumn and the pond frozen in the winter, the 'donkey derby', taking my puppy for walks and eventually it was the place I 'ran away' to when I was told we were moving away from Farnborough!

Sarah Steadman

Farnborough, The Park c1965 F9213

Teenage Memories of Cove in the 1950s

Cove was a special place, a place where I was born, at 11 Sydney Smith Close.

My grandad, Matthew Smith, lived at 39 Holly Road and worked on the railway as a plate layer. When I was growing up in the 1950s we lived in Hazel Avenue, and I spent all my childhood spare time on Eelmoor Farm with Uncle Eddy Arrow. It was a great time for me, he was the local woodman and also kept pigs, we used to do a swill round in RAF Borough. Later on I worked as a delivery boy for the local shop, J E King and Son, also known locally as 'Cookies' because Jim Cook was the father of Joan King. When I delivered groceries around RAF Borough, if the

> "He was the local woodman and also kept pigs..."

householder wasn't at home I used to let myself into the house, place the groceries on the table and pick up my money from the table where a row of money would have been left out, for the groceries, the milkman, the tallyman etc. That was when the world was full of trust, it wouldn't happen today!

Peter Smith

Passing by the Elephant & Castle...

As a young child living in Farnborough in the 1950s
I remember feeling so scared as I walked past the
Elephant and Castle pub in Lynchford Road, as often
there would stand an old man in a long black coat and
a black hat, and he would very slowly shake his finger
at me. Whether it was just at me or any passing child I
never knew, but it used to frighten the life out of me!

Julia Clarke

Farnborough, Lynchford Road c1955   F9020

That was my parents' shop!

This photograph of Bridge Road in Cove clearly shows The Cove Supply Stores building on the right. My parents ran that shop from about 1936 to 1945. The Bridge Road end of the shop in the photo was the off-licence. Opposite the shop on Cove Road was the Ivy Leaf Club. I have such memories of Cove. I attended the Hawley Road Elementary School, and remember one teacher well, a Mr Harold Crapper, who was a devil with the cane! Later I attended Farnborough Grammar School.

I wonder whether anyone can remember Mr Thornton's menswear shop, which was opposite Mr Munday's newsagency? He used to place an advert in the local paper which always included a little poem referring to 'Thornton's Bib-and-Brace'. Mr Munday's newsagency was always popular with boys and girls because of the comics he sold. If I remember rightly, there was a battery-charging and bicycle shop on the corner of Hazel Avenue run by a Mr Young.

> "I remember one teacher well, a Mr Harold Crapper, who was a devil with the cane!"

I remember that I \used to check the 'B' button in the public phone box near the Post Office on Bridge Road to see if anyone had forgotten to get their money back – sometimes I was lucky and found tuppence!

Ronald Catmur

Cove, Bridge Road c1955 C172009

A little book of memories

Fleet – my hometown

I was born and raised in the Fleet area. My dad (Leonard) had a shop in the High Street. I knew this area well and I remember the milk bar where me and my friends went for milkshakes. We used to go to school in Farnborough by steam train, we had to walk down to the station and catch the train to Farnborough. It was lovely when it was good weather, but not so nice in the rain and snow!

My mum used to take me to Mr Cane's shop to get the groceries and he would deliver them. There were hams and sausages hanging from the ceiling, and bacon and cheese were cut in front of you – the taste was out of this world. There was sawdust on the floor, and the shop had a lovely smell. There was so much to see in his shop that you couldn't take it all in at first.

Rosemary Prime

Fleet, Fleet Road c1965   F32029

Growing up on Velmead Farm at Church Crookham

In the 1960s my father was cowman on Velmead Farm, Watery Lane, Church Crookham, we lived in the tythe cottage on the farm for about 6 years. I started school in the village, my teacher was Mrs War whose husband was the foreman of Velmead Farm. At the time I had 2 sisters who were older than me and 3 brothers who were younger. We walked across the fields to school. It was a lovely, idyllic place to live as a child, we had so much freedom. We used to go to Saturday morning pictures in Fleet, crossing the canal over a rickety bridge that would

> "It was a lovely, idyllic place to live as a child, we had so much freedom."

have not passed today's Health & Safety rules. We had a well in the garden for our water supply – our father would draw 2 buckets in the morning before he went to work and 2 more when he came in at mid-day for his dinner, and then again at teatime. Life was very hard but we knew no better.

Doreen Bonner

A little book of memories

Saturday morning pictures at Aldershot

Seeing this photograph of Aldershot's High Street on the Frith website brought back memories of my regular Saturday morning trips to the pictures in the late 1940s and early 50s. In Aldershot we were lucky that the Empire (an Odeon cinema) and the Ritz (an ABC cinema) were situated right next to each other, the two large buildings seen in this view. We looked at each programme displayed and, depending on which film we fancied, chose the one we wanted to see. It certainly gave our mums an hour or so without having to amuse their kids at weekends! Imagine the despair if we were too ill to attend one week and had to miss the next exciting episode of 'Flash Gordon' or other gripping serial instalments. My most vivid memories are of the huge ruched curtains in front of the screen which went up at the start of the show, and of horrid boys who kept clambering over the seats or threw their sweet wrappers at us girls. We kids used to sing the 'Odeon song' at the beginning of the Saturday morning pictures – we sang it as loud as we could, and the noise was deafening!

Diana Lawer

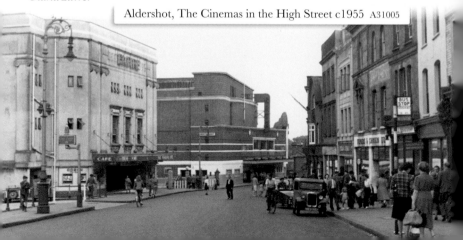

Aldershot, The Cinemas in the High Street c1955 A31005

The dramatic consequences of dancing lessons at the NAAFI Club!

It was 1952 and the NAAFI Club at Aldershot for Armed Forces servicemen based at the local barracks held dancing lessons. Now, trying to learn to dance in hobnailed Army boots was impossible, but I did chat up a NAAFI girl and arranged to meet her after her work, which I did. She had, to me, an exotic name and was Finnish. When I arrived back at Badajos Barracks the Intelligence Corps awaited me. I was taken to their HQ near Tunbridge Wells and quizzed overnight. Apparently they thought she was a Soviet spy and had been placed there to quiz soldiers about their regiments! I was so innocent then, but was angry when they refused me transport back to Aldershot. I had to phone the RSM who reluctantly sent a PU vehicle for me to return to Aldershot and my RASC unit. Being the RSM he really tore me off a strip – as RSMs do, of course – but as he dismissed me, with an angry warning about chatting up foreign girls and wasting his time, he winked.

Graham Vahey

Aldershot, The NAAFI Club c1960 A31083

A little book of memories

School dinners, frozen milk and Abbot and Costello

1948 was the year I started at Kingsley School. We lived in Oakhanger, but at the Shortheath Common end so to Kingsley I went, on the back of my mother's bike. School dinners came in hay boxes delivered in the back of a Landrover from wherever – I remember lots of stews and cabbage. In the winter, our bottles of frozen milk were put next to the large fire at the end of the schoolroom to thaw out.

This photograph shows the Cricketers Arms at Kingsley. We used to go around the back of the pub and watch 'Abbott and Costello' on their very small black and white TV, built into a very large box.

Ian Quinnell

Kingsley, The Village 1933 85761

Hampshire

I was stationed at Bordon Army Fire Station

was a Corporal in the Army in the late 1940s and was stationed at Bordon Fire Station. I was in charge of the cook-house and also of the bar on the Fire Station. I attended many fires, the biggest was the Honky Tonk (its Army name), which burnt to the ground. We were given its wrong name, the night was very foggy, and the address we were given was the Bagshot and Bordon Soldiers' Home, so we set off and went to Bagshot. We had no radio or other way of getting information, and we phoned Bordon when we got to Bagshot Army Camp and found no fire there, and were told to come back to Bordon. By the time we returned, the National Fire Service was there. We had to watch the fire burn out as there was a limited supply of water. Incidentally, the sixpenny bits in the 'one-arm bandits' were fused together. I also attended the forest fire which burned for 3 weeks before the rain came to help put it out. It burnt to 3 foot deep in the ground.   *Laurence Brocklesby*

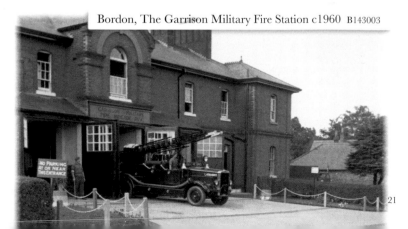

Bordon, The Garrison Military Fire Station c1960 B143003

21

A walk down memory lane in Headley

Oh my… when I looked at the Headley photos on the Frith website, this one certainly brought back memories. This was my old school in the 1950s. There was a lane at the side of the school which eventually led to our home, and I remember that one day my sister and I decided to walk home along it, without a care in the world. Unfortunately, our mom was waiting for the school bus at the other end of the lane, and you can imagine how worried she was when we weren't on it. Well, you can guess what sort of reception we got when we arrived in tow with the policeman sent out to look for us, what a memory…

Viviane Holding

Headley, Headley Holme School c1955 H60001

Beech Hill Corner at Headley Down

I remember this place so well, this is the bus stop I used to get from Mill Chase School in the 1960s. Many an ugly scrap would occur on the school bus with the kids from the Erie Camp, I think behind the bus shelter in this view is one of the old Army huts the families lived in. I lived at Ludshott Grove in the new houses opposite Erie Camp. I remember a good old local copper called PC Pike, he was a great old soul who used to give us a clip around the ear for scrumping the apples from the orchard near the deep pond at the bottom of Beech Hill. Those were the days.

Stuart Scott

Headley Down, Beech Hill Corner c1955   H415006

Singing my way to Soberton in the 1950s

My mum used to bike over from North Boarhunt to Soberton every Thursday when I was small. She had a small seat fixed at the back of the bike so she could take me too, but I had to sit on a blanket as it was hard. The journey used to take a while and I would sit back there and sing my heart out. As I was so small, people could not see me until we had gone past, and I am sure they thought it was my mum singing. We used to go to the end of Trampers Lane to join Church Road, turn left and go past Newtown school, then turn first right into Ingoldfield Lane to Soberton. Those lanes were narrow and the fields either side were higher than the road, and when it snowed they were impassable.

> "I will always remember her with her skirt held up, picking the wild watercress in the river."

My nan lived at the 'Five Trees' at Soberton in a cottage, it was one of five, and the river ran out by her front. When there was flooding, if it wasn't for the step that led up to the front door, we would have been paddling. There was a railway line up the bank in front and to the side and I just about remember the last trains that passed there. I used to love going there to visit my nan, who sadly passed away in 1976. I will always remember her with her skirt held up, picking the wild watercress in the river. She always said that if you picked anything from the river, you should do it upstream from the cows, at the time I could not understand why – but I do now.   *Vanessa Hillman (née Miles)*

I was in the very first intake to this school

Denmead Primary School had just been built and I was in the class of 1960. I struggle to recall the teachers' names but I'm pretty sure there was a Miss Lynn and there was definitely a Miss Kill. She was my first love at the age of five! By a quirk of the internet I met online a 'girl' from my former class, now in her 50s, who was still in touch with Miss Kill and I was able to get a message to her. Incredibly, some 48 years and a thousand-plus pupils later she still remembered ME! I remember running across that grassy area in the photograph on a very stormy day at around the time the view was taken. I was (almost) convinced that if I ran fast enough into the wind it would pick me up on my mackintosh wings and I would fly. I remember it very clearly.

Graham Willers

Denmead, The Primary School c1960 D181050

Memories of old Cowplain

We were the first family to move into the newly built Padnell
Avenue Council Estate at Cowplain, moving there in around 1947.
Our house was one of a pair on the corner of Winscombe Avenue.
I lived there until I married my wife Maureen at St Wilfred's
Church, Padnell Road in 1971. I have many fond memories of
the area and I'm sure other people of Cowplain will share my
memories of Padnell Recreation Ground, 'The Swamps', 'The
Humps & Bumps', going to the Bon-Bon shop at the top of
Padnell for sweets (seen on the left of photograph C576008
below), 'Joey's Field', the lily pond, the boat pond, and the 'Tanks' in
the Queen's Inclosure. Then there was the farm pond at Padnell
Farm where we would spend hours fishing for sticklebacks and
the golf course – we would spend hours there causing havoc
with the golfers, and also wading barefoot in the golf course
pond feeling for lost balls that we would then attempt to sell
back to the players.

Cowplain, London Road c1960   C576008

I also remember Bert Steer's Transport Café at the top of Latchmore Forest Grove and the Cowplain Boys' Club up towards Lovedean Corner. Then there was Fodens Garage at the top of Park Lane, the hardware shop, Coxons newsagents where my sister Shirley worked for a short while, the Post Office in Kings Road, and Gauntlets the grocer which was next to the milk depot run by Mr Watford who delivered his milk by horse and cart, I would sometimes help him on his round. Then there was the Mission at the end of Mission Lane, Les Simpson the barber, Patterson the greengrocer, Chapman's Laundry (seen in photograph C567033 below), Hood the cobbler, Carter's sweet shop and at the end of Durley Avenue there was Tumblers, selling TVs, records and push bikes. Prior to it being Tumblers I can remember it being Kimble's Tea Shop. Sadly I can also remember the demolition for house building of the Hazleton Woods, and the construction of the Wecock Farm Estate, the Cherry Tree Estate in Park Lane (now Tempest Avenue), the Highfield Farm Estate and the A3(M) motorway that ploughed its way right through the idyllic countryside that was our playground as kids. *Michael Dewey*

Cowplain, London Road c1965 C576033

A little book of memories

The sign of the Spotted Cow...

My grandmother lived in Idsworth Road in Cowplain. When I was a small boy we used to drive down from Scotland to spend summer and Christmas holidays with her. Seeing the pub sign of the Spotted Cow at Cowplain was a cause of great excitement for a 4-year-old because it meant we were nearly there. At that time Idsworth Road was not tarmacked and the surface was very rough. My dad used to sit me on his knees and let me steer the car round the potholes.

Jon Rose

Cowplain, The Spotted Cow c1965 C576025

Childhood memories of wartime Havant

In the early 1940s I went to Manor House School in Havant. It was run by Dr and Mrs Wallace, and occupied the former rectory in South Street (the site is now covered by a housing estate and the motorway to Portsmouth). Fr Williams was one of the best teachers I ever had: absolutely inspiring. Madame Worrell, the doughty French mistress, was a familiar sight around town riding her massive tricycle. You didn't argue with Madame Worrell. This was during the Second World War and the area around Havant and Hayling Island experienced frequent attacks from the Luftwaffe (from both bomber aircraft and flying bombs, known as 'dooglebugs') and many a night I spent sheltering in the cellar of our home at 31 East Street listening to the sounds of screaming dive-bombers, anti-aircraft guns, and shrapnel falling around us, or standing at my bedroom window watching doodlebugs flying past on their way towards London. If the flame from a doodlebug's jet engine went out, you knew you had just a few seconds to take cover before it hit the ground and exploded. There was an anti-aircraft battery between Farlington and Bedhampton which always put up a spirited defence against the Luftwaffe.

I remember the massive build-up of troops and vehicles in the surrounding countryside just prior to the D-Day invasion on June 1944. The whole area was sealed off from non-residents and there was even a special alert for German spies in the area.

We also savoured some of the triumphs of our own Armed Forces, such as the return of the Dieppe Raid heroes in 1942 (I saw them waving their captured Nazi flags as their troop train passed through Havant station) and the great air armada of towed gliders on their way to Normandy to pave the way for the D-Day landings. It made you proud to be British.   *Barry Mahony*

A little book of memories

Swimming from the Victoria Pier at Portsmouth

In the 1950s and 60s the outfall from the power station made the water warm here so that we swam all year round – although it was not safe for those who didn't know the currents. Visitors to Portsmouth who watched us were amazed at our apparent hardiness, or perhaps foolhardiness.

Frank Stratford

Portsmouth, Victoria Pier and the Sally Port c1960 P100067

The Portsmouth mudlarks

When I was a child in the 1950s, when we used to go down to the Sally Port at Portsmouth there were often a lot of local 'urchins' there who were called 'the mudlarks'. They used to stand in the knee-deep, sloppy black mud below the pier to the ferry when the tide was out and people would throw them pennies which they had to find in the mud. They'd end up covered in mud from head to foot. A lot of them were great characters and had developed great 'carny' skills to get people to toss them money.   *Dylan Rivis*

My father was one of those mudlarks!

My father was one of those so-called 'mudlarks' of Portsmouth mentioned in the memory by Dylan Rivis (above). I remember him telling me stories of how they used to stage mock fights over the pennies to make people feel sorry for them and throw more money. Any thought that the mudlarks were poor orphans who had to do this to stay alive was very far from the truth. My father's family lived very well in a house in Southsea near the Kings Theatre.

The memory of his boyhood antics was brought back to me on a recent trip to Egypt and a cruise down the Nile. Children beg for money along the banks of the Nile as the cruiser goes by at the narrow points. After the ship is gone, they get their BMX bikes out of the bushes and pedal away to the mud brick house where they live, with the satellite dish on the roof and the Merc parked outside.

Darryl Thorne

A little book of memories

The Art Exhibition, Old Portsmouth

My grandparents, Bert and Dorrie Hedger, started this amateur art exhibition at Portsmouth in about 1965, and carried on until my grandfather died in 1982. I recognise several of the paintings in this photograph as being by my mum, Rita Grant, as I was taken down there every weekend from the age of three.

Christopher Grant

Portsmouth, Artist's Corner, The Sally Port c1965 P100065

"Somewhere beyond the sea... my lover waits for me..."

As a young lad I had great eyesight for long distances. As we sat on the pebbled beach at Southsea in the 1950s it was always me that first spotted a slight bump on the horizon as the then huge incoming passenger ocean liners such as the 'Queen Mary', 'Queen Elizabeth', 'Mauretania' and many more returning from New York came down the Solent back towards their home port of Southampton. I enjoyed being scoffed at for a good half hour or more before the others managed to notice the liners approaching, with the telltale wisp of smoke from their funnels.

Later on I worked during one summer holiday as a waiter at the Seaview Hotel on the Isle of Wight, where we got a grandstand view of those great ships sailing by. I had my first kiss on the seawall at Seaview when a lovely Dutch girl called Riet Berendsen took a fancy to me. How great was that as the sun set and the ships sailed by? I wonder where she is now...

Dylan Rivis

Portmouth, RMS 'Queen Mary' c1955 P100001

A little book of memories

Just like yesterday!

Wow, seeing this awesome photograph (H40021 below) transports me back in time because in the same year this was taken I would have been taking this very ferry over to Hayling Island from the Southsea side, after taking the trolley bus and regular bus to the ferry point from my home in North End in Portsmouth.

Some of our group would drive with my Aunty Linda in her old Austin (with the canvas fold-down roof) around to Hayling by road, carrying all the sandwiches, blankets and other beach paraphernalia. I always opted for the ferry trip as I loved stepping off the dock down into the ferry which had bench seats alongside the gunwales. Sometimes I would stand riding the swell as we swung out into the heavy running tide. I was in my element with the wind streaming through my hair and the smell of the marshes in my nostrils.

Upon reaching the other shore we had a pretty long walk to the spot where we settled down into the dunes next to the old golf club building, away from all the nasty holidaymaker stuff in the town. There would be some pretty heavy seas coming into Hayling at high tide, what with there being a sandy bottom, but we had a lot of fun diving through the pounding 6-8ft waves as they came onshore, all under the watchful eye of my step-grandfather, Pop, or my Aunty Linda.   *Dylan Rivis*

Hayling Island, The Ferry c1955   H400021

Hampshire

Bag carrying on Hayling Island

I remember waiting at the bus stop at the bottom
of Creek Road on Hayling Island with an old pram
so I could take incoming holidaymakers and their
bags to their bungalow for a very small fee. I was
still at school at the time.

Ralph Rushton

Hayling Island, Creek Road c1960 H400038

A little book of memories

The dancing years at Lee Tower

In 1953 I was stationed at HMS 'Ariel' (the radio school attached to HMS 'Daedalus') and went dancing in the Tower ballroom at Lee-on-the-Solent every Wednesday night. It was a wonderful place, and I met my wife there! At that time she lived at Sarisbury Green and had to leave the dance early to catch the local bus connection to Sarisbury Green via Titchfield – for some time I always used to wonder where she had vanished to! It took weeks before I could eventually see her home...

Robert Andrew

Lee-on-the-Solent, Lee Tower c1955 L461001

Hampshire

Up the Tower at Lee-on-the-Solent

I went up the Tower at Lee-on-the-Solent at some time in the 1950s. I paid all of sixpence at the little kiosk just inside the entrance, then a lift whisked us up to the top. I am so glad that I did it as I have a wonderful memory of the view from the top of the tower. It was a beautiful day so you could see for miles. What an attraction that tower would be today.

Opened in 1935, the 120ft Art Deco tower afforded views across the Solent to the Isle of Wight, and hosted a cinema, restaurant and ballroom. Deemed unsafe, the complex was demolished by 1971.

Gaynor Boyd

Lee-on-the-Solent, The View from Lee Tower c1960   L461025

The animals on Fareham's market day

My memory of Fareham dates from the 1960s, when on market day the town's market was filled with pigs, sheep, cattle, chickens etc. I remember watching in awe as the cattle were walked through High Street and West Street to the market (now a car park), and standing up on the temporary fencing so I could reach over to stroke the sheep, and hearing the market auction man selling the cows; to this day I never understood a word he said, but they all got sold somehow. I can still remember the smell of the market – there were no rubber gloves and handwashes in those days, but it didn't do me any harm, just gave me great memories! My visit to the market was always followed by a trip to good old 'Soothills' bakers' shop in East Street for their famous pasties and lardy cakes! Soothills in Fareham is still going strong and is just as popular (if not more) these days.

Jean Oxtoby (née Wigmore)

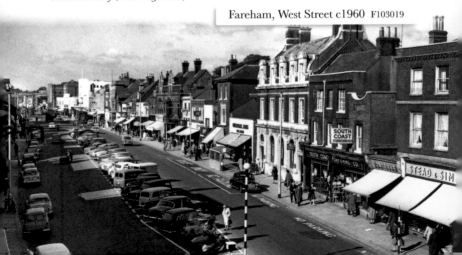

Fareham, West Street c1960 F103019

Ragworming at Fareham in the 1960s

I used to go to the 'Creek' at Fareham (as it was called then) with my father, where we would join a whole host of bait diggers. The main bait we were looking for was ragworms, which are a bit like centipedes but they bite! This ... the creek became polluted, mind you. On one occasion my wellington boots ended up stuck in the mud and as I tried to walk (totally unsuccessful) I ended up falling face first into the mud, I ended up caked in mud from head to toe and it absolutely stank! My mother was not amused, venting her displeasure not just at me in my misfortune but also at my father who, in her words, had "let it happen".

Jean Oxtoby (née Wigmore)

Fareham, The Harbour c1960 F103024

Memories of the 'children's hospital' at Bursledon

In 1948 Brixedone House at Bursledon was bought by the Southampton Children's Hospital to become the 'Bursledon Annexe', a convalescent home for children where they could receive some schooling as well as medical care. This grand country house was formerly the home of the Thistlethwaite family. It remained in service as a children's convalescent home until 1989, when the Bursledon Annexe was closed and the NHS sold Brixedone House.

Bursledon, The Hospital c1955 B304049

I remember being a patient at this hospital in the early 1950s, I was placed there for convalescence, following being in Great Ormond Street Hospital for several years as I was a very sick child. I clearly remember my father coming to collect me to take me home to Southampton on his bicycle.

Leonard Hughes

This is just how I remember the hospital which I first went into it in 1956 as a child with kidney failure. I stayed there for 7 years, until 1963. It was an annexe for long-term patients from Southampton Children's Hospital, staffed by brilliant nurses and doctors. My consultant was Dr Williamson who undoubtedly saved my life. It was a marvellous place and I have many memories from those days, including a visit by Billy Smart's Circus, taking my 11 plus examination on my own in an upstairs room, being close to death and wheeled into the hall to be more quiet, then having my going up ceremony from Cubs to Scouts in the grounds of the hospital. The staff were magnificent. I particularly remember Nurse Chum, who had a finger missing, and Nurse Hayward, who all the young boys were in love with. Here I am aged 58 and still here thanks to those great people.

Tim Manhire

I was here in November 1965 after having rheumatic fever. I remember being in a ward which was second on the right off the great entrance hall where we ate and were allowed to watch telly some evenings, if we were good. I recall watching 'Batman' there! I think my ward was a ten bed ward with a large cot in the bay window. The ward for babies was upstairs and we were sometimes allowed to help feed them. On a Sunday we had to attend a religious service in the hall. This was the only day other children could visit us, such as our brothers and sisters.

Tina Alldridge

A little book of memories

Southampton old and new

The Bargate at Southampton was originally built to guard the main road into the medieval town. Over the years it has been a toll-gate, a prison, a guildhall and a museum. The original Norman arch dates back to about 1175, and the tower was added a century later. The upper floor used to be a guildhall. This early photograph shows the Bargate at its best. Characterised by pointed arches and fine stonework, the old gate is also renowned for its statue of George III gazing down the High Street, dressed in Classical style as a Roman and wearing a toga. The Bargate is one of the finest medieval gateways in the country, dating back to the late 12th century. Until the 1930s, specially designed trams travelled through the Bargate, with dome-shaped tops to fit the arch. The adjoining walls and buildings were subsequently destroyed so that traffic bypassed the gate. The area north of the Bargate is known as Above Bar.

Southampton, The Bargate 1908   60428

Above Bar after the war

We moved to Southampton in early 1950 just after the trams had stopped running – some of the rails were still there. Above Bar, along with much of Southampton, had been badly bombed in the Second World War and there were still many bomb sites on both sides of the road. Woolworth's was a large wooden hut reached by a bridge across a crater. Gradually during the 1950s new buildings sprang up amid the bomb sites until the scene was as in this 1960 picture. The Odeon cinema and building next to it had survived the war but most of the rest was new. Owing to shortages of building materials after the war some of the new buildings were not of the best quality and now 50-plus years later some of their exteriors are already showing their age.

Revel Partington

Southampton, Above Bar c1960 S151181

Fun on the ferry home from Southampton

Around about 1956-57 we would all go to dances or parties in Southampton. The last bus back to our homes in Hythe/Holbury/Fawley/Calshot was about 10.30pm and inevitably we girls missed it, so there was always a mad dash through Southampton to the docks to get the last ferry across Southampton Water to Hythe, which went about 10.45pm, I think. The skipper had always cast off but the harbour police who were nearby used to yell out to him and the ferry would tread water, so to speak, and the police would pick us up in their boat and throw us on board the ferry. It was such good fun, but I expect Health and Safety would frown mightily on such antics now! We would recite Shakespeare, much adulterated, to give the other ferry passengers a laugh and generally play about being silly. I remember one night

> "I was lucky enough to get asked backstage where I met Buddy and his band, the Crickets"

when after going to a Buddy Holly concert at Southampton I got left behind by the rest of the group, but I was lucky enough to get asked backstage where I met Buddy and his band, the Crickets; they drew little cartoon bugs all over my arm around the moles and freckles. I had to sprint for the ferry that night and the other girls were so envious when I caught up with the bus at Hythe and showed off my arm. Golly, I didn't wash that arm for a month! Alas, sometimes we missed both the bus and the ferry – believe me, it was a long hike home to Fawley in stiletto heels…   *Jeannette Lomas*

HOTSPUR III
SOUTHAMPTON

Hythe, The Ferry c1960 H372077

The Bakery in the High Street

Who else remembers the smell of that freshly baked
bread coming from the bakery in Milford on Sea's
High Street, the flat-roofed building seen on the left
of this photograph with the 'Hovis' sign outside? As I
child in the 1960s I would volunteer to go to the baker's
and rush home with that hot, freshly baked loaf and
devour both crusts.

Rex Harrod

Milford on Sea, High Street c1960   M303158

Hampshire

Childhood memories of New Milton

I remember exploring the back streets of New Milton, Ashley, Bashley and Barton on Sea on my bike as a young boy in the 1960s. Phelps supermarket was our mum's main food shopping weekly destination. Burgess News Agency was where she would buy us our weekly comics. My siblings and myself would cherish our weekly read. I had 'Topper' while my brothers and sister had 'Beano', 'Victor' and 'Tammy'. I remember the excitement of unwrapping the comic annuals from our Christmas stocking each year. Our Hornby

> "I had 'Topper' while my brothers and sister had 'Beano', 'Victor' and 'Tammy'."

trainset would often see the dining room's daylight but not as much as my brother's Britain's farm set! We all at some stage went to New Milton Junior School and two of us went to Gore Road Secondary School (now Arnewood) before emigrating to Australia in 1970. Ballard Lake was the place to trial my eldest brother's model motor boat, where the ducks were as intrigued as we were! The local recreation ground would often be the place to vent our football enthusiasm. My brother and I used to challenge each other with football collection memorabilia, from cards of players in the First Division to Esso commemorative bronze coins of the English World Cup squad in 1970. I also remember getting the bumper stickers from the local Esso garage emblazoned with the 'Tiger in your Tank' branding. The distinctive smell of screen print inks was memorable.   _Colin Burnell_

The Local Bobby

In 1932 my policeman father Len James was moved to Brockenhurst
in the New Forest as the 'village bobby'. We lived in the Police
House (now a renovated private home) and eventually both my
brother (born 1929) and I (born 1931) went to the local C of E primary
school. Almost next door to the Police House was a sweet shop,
and I remember that a cone of lollies cost a halfpenny. Dad had a
standard issue police bicycle, on which he would ride to Lyndhurst
and submit his report to the Station Sergeant there, then in 1934 we
bought a 1928 Morris Minor car, which seemed an absolute luxury.
With the New Forest a short walk away, our boyhood days were
magical. I can remember picking gorse flowers, bottling them in
water and selling them as perfume. On one occasion a New Forest
pony was born on the common opposite the Police House, and we
were fascinated to watch the episode and to see how quickly the
little foal struggled to its feet. Gypsy caravans came to the village
occasionally and Dad would be out and about to monitor their
activities, but there was never any trouble.

In 1939 Dad was promoted to a Sergeant and transferred to
Eastleigh in time for the start of the Second World War.   *Len James*

Brockenhurst, A Delivery Cart in the Village 1949 B394007

This was my uncle's butcher's shop

Although in 1949 the sign over the front of the butcher's shop next to the Foresters Arms pub in this view showed the name 'Gosling', at the time this photograph was taken it was in fact owned by my uncle, Albert Parker. Albert lived in the house attached to the shop, named 'New Forest Villas', with his wife Florence, their two sons Albert and Stanley and two daughters, Dorothy and Marjorie. The house and business were sold following the death of Uncle Bert

> "I remember placing halfpenny coins on the railway track at the level crossing."

in 1964. I spent many happy holidays in Brockenhurst as a boy, staying with my aunt and uncle. I remember placing halfpenny coins on the railway track at the level crossing in the village, trying to make them into one penny coins when a passing train squashed them – but I never got rich!   *Oliver Barnes*

Brockenhurst, Brookley Road 1949 B394004

A little book of memories

The missing archway of the Grand Hotel at Lyndhurst

My mother told me that the two white pillars at the entrance to the Grand Hotel at Lyndhurst once supported an archway. During the Second World War the Royal Navy billeted personnel in the hotel who were bused out each day. The bus was too tall to go under the archway and so they decided to blow up the arch. The resulting explosion shattered every window in the hotel and was heard all over the village!

Maggie Barnes

Lyndhurst, The Grand Hotel c1955   L123039

I was born in the Post Office at Nether Wallop

I was born in the Post Office at Nether Wallop, the house in the background of this view. My father Oliver Hinwood was postmaster there from 1903 to 1961. He used to take photographs of the village and send them to the Frith company to be developed and then sold the postcards in the shop. The photograph shows the garage where we kept our car and to the side of that was a bakehouse where bread was baked daily. The person walking towards the shop in this view is the Reverend Frank Walter Hyne-Davy, who was vicar of Nether Wallop at that time.

> "The person walking towards the shop is the Reverend Frank Walter Hyne-Davy, who was vicar of Nether Wallop."

Mrs Eileen Wilmott

Nether Wallop, The Square c1955 N156001

FRANCIS FRITH

PIONEER   VICTORIAN   PHOTOGRAPHER

Francis Frith, founder of the world-famous photographic archive, was a complex and multi-talented man. A devout Quaker and a highly successful Victorian businessman, he was philosophical by nature and pioneering in outlook. By 1855 he had already established a wholesale grocery business in Liverpool, and sold it for the astonishing sum of £200,000, which is the equivalent today of over £15,000,000. Now in his thirties, and captivated by the new science of photography, Frith set out on a series of pioneering journeys up the Nile and to the Near East.

INTRIGUE AND EXPLORATION

He was the first photographer to venture beyond the sixth cataract of the Nile. Africa was still the mysterious 'Dark Continent', and Stanley and Livingstone's historic meeting was a decade into the future. The conditions for picture taking confound belief. He laboured for hours in his wicker dark-room in the sweltering heat of the desert, while the volatile chemicals fizzed dangerously in their trays. Back in London he exhibited his photographs and was 'rapturously cheered' by members of the Royal Society. His reputation as a photographer was made overnight.

VENTURE OF A LIFE-TIME

By the 1870s the railways had threaded their way across the country, and Bank Holidays and half-day Saturdays had been made obligatory by Act of Parliament. All of a sudden the working man and his family were able to enjoy days out, take holidays, and see a little more of the world.

With typical business acumen, Francis Frith foresaw that these new tourists would enjoy having souvenirs to commemorate their days out. For the next thirty years he travelled the country by train and by pony and trap, producing fine photographs of seaside resorts and beauty spots that were keenly bought by millions of Victorians. These prints were painstakingly pasted into family albums and pored over during the dark nights of winter, rekindling precious memories of summer excursions. Frith's studio was soon supplying retail shops all over the country, and by 1890 F Frith & Co had become the greatest specialist photographic publishing company in the world, with over 2,000 sales outlets, and pioneered the picture postcard.

FRANCIS FRITH'S LEGACY

Francis Frith had died in 1898 at his villa in Cannes, his great project still growing. By 1970 the archive he created contained over a third of a million pictures showing 7,000 British towns and villages.

Frith's legacy to us today is of immense significance and value, for the magnificent archive of evocative photographs he created provides a unique record of change in the cities, towns and villages throughout Britain over a century and more. Frith and his fellow studio photographers revisited locations many times down the years to update their views, compiling for us an enthralling and colourful pageant of British life and character.

We are fortunate that Frith was dedicated to recording the minutiae of everyday life. For it is this sheer wealth of visual data, the painstaking chronicle of changes in dress, transport, street layouts, buildings, housing and landscape that captivates us so much today, offering us a powerful link with the past and with the lives of our ancestors.

Computers have now made it possible for Frith's many thousands of images to be accessed almost instantly. The archive offers every one of us an opportunity to examine the places where we and our families have lived and worked down the years. Its images, depicting our shared past, are now bringing pleasure and enlightenment to millions around the world a century and more after his death.

For further information visit: www.francisfrith.com

INTERIOR DECORATION

Frith's photographs can be seen framed and as giant wall murals in thousands of pubs, restaurants, hotels, banks, retail stores and other public buildings throughout Britain. These provide interesting and attractive décor, generating strong local interest and acting as a powerful reminder of gentler days in our increasingly busy and frenetic world.

FRITH PRODUCTS

All Frith photographs are available as prints and posters in a variety of different sizes and styles. In the UK we also offer a range of other gift and stationery products illustrated with Frith photographs, although many of these are not available for delivery outside the UK – see our web site for more information on the products available for delivery in your country.

THE INTERNET

Over 100,000 photographs of Britain can be viewed and purchased on the Frith web site. The web site also includes memories and reminiscences contributed by our customers, who have personal knowledge of localities and of the people and properties depicted in Frith photographs. If you wish to learn more about a specific town or village you may find these reminiscences fascinating to browse. Why not add your own comments if you think they would be of interest to others? See **www.francisfrith.com**

PLEASE HELP US BRING FRITH'S PHOTOGRAPHS TO LIFE

Our authors do their best to recount the history of the places they write about. They give insights into how particular towns and villages developed, they describe the architecture of streets and buildings, and they discuss the lives of famous people who lived there. But however knowledgeable our authors are, the story they tell is necessarily incomplete.

Frith's photographs are so much more than plain historical documents. They are living proofs of the flow of human life down the generations. They show real people at real moments in history; and each of those people is the son or daughter of someone, the brother or sister, aunt or uncle, grandfather or grandmother of someone else. All of them lived, worked and played in the streets depicted in Frith's photographs.

We would be grateful if you would give us your insights into the places shown in our photographs: the streets and buildings, the shops, businesses and industries. Post your memories of life in those streets on the Frith website: what it was like growing up there, who ran the local shop and what shopping was like years ago; if your workplace is shown tell us about your working day and what the building is used for now. Read other visitors' memories and reconnect with your shared local history and heritage. With your help more and more Frith photographs can be brought to life, and vital memories preserved for posterity, and for the benefit of historians in the future.

Wherever possible, we will try to include some of your comments in future editions of our books. Moreover, if you spot errors in dates, titles or other facts, please let us know, because our archive records are not always completely accurate—they rely on 140 years of human endeavour and hand-compiled records. You can email us using the contact form on the website.

Thank you!

For further information, trade, or author enquiries
please contact us at the address below:

**The Francis Frith Collection, 6 Oakley Business Park,
Wylye Road, Dinton, Wiltshire SP3 5EU.**
Tel: +44 (0)1722 716 376 Fax: +44 (0)1722 716 881
e-mail: sales@francisfrith.co.uk **www.francisfrith.com**